S0-AQC-887

Poochie's Place

By Eve Bunting

Illustrated by Patricia Ludlow

⌐Ɔ Dominie Press, Inc.

Publisher: Raymond Yuen
Project Editor: John S. F. Graham
Editor: Bob Rowland
Designer: Greg DiGenti
Illustrator: Patricia Ludlow

Text Copyright © 2003 Eve Bunting
Illustrations Copyright © 2003 Dominie Press, Inc.
All rights reserved. No part of this publication may
be reproduced or transmitted in any form or by any
means without permission in writing from the publisher.
Reproduction of any part of this book, through photocopy,
recording, or any electronic or mechanical retrieval system,
without the written permission of the publisher, is an
infringement of the copyright law.

Published by:

℘ Dominie Press, Inc.

1949 Kellogg Avenue
Carlsbad, California 92008 USA

www.dominie.com

1-800-232-4570

Paperback ISBN 0-7685-2062-2
Printed in Singapore by PH Productions Pte Ltd
1 2 3 4 5 6 PH 05 04 03

Table of Contents

Chapter One
Poochie Has to Learn

Today I got a puppy. Her name is
Poochie, and I love her already. Dad and
I bought her a green collar and a green
leash and a green doggie dish. Then Dad
saw a basket with a little house over it.

"We'll get this for her," he said.

Poochie and I were worried. "We don't have to keep her outside, do we?" I asked.

Dad shook his head. "No. This will be her house inside our house," he said. "In our kitchen."

Poochie and I smiled. "All right then."

When we got home, my dog and I played in the garden. I chased her and she chased me. I showed her the oak tree that our fat opossum climbs. I showed her the bluebird's nest in the old elm.

"You'll have lots of friends," I promised.

I gave Poochie her supper in her new green dish. Her ears fell in her food, and I sponged them off.

We set her doggie house in the kitchen, and Dad made a wooden sign to hang above her door. Poochie's Place, it said.

That night, at bedtime, we put her in

her basket. She climbed out and ran to me.

"I think she should sleep in my bed tonight," I said. "Please, please!"

Mom and Dad looked at each other. "OK," Mom said. "But just for this first night. We don't want that to become a habit."

So Poochie and I snuggled together in bed, all warm and cozy.

But the next night they put her in Poochie's Place again. They switched out the light. They closed the kitchen door. Poochie began scratching at the door and barking little yappy barks.

"Poor Poochie," I said. "Please let her come up with me."

Dad shook his head. "I don't think so," he said. "Poochie has to learn."

I felt like crying as I ran up to bed.

Chapter Two

This Is the Very Last Time

I lay in bed with my fingers in my ears.

Then I took them out and listened hard. I heard the kitchen door open. I heard Mom say, "Be quiet, little Poochie."

Then I heard Dad say, "Poochie! You rascal! Come back here!"

There was a *scamper, scamper, scamper* on the stairs. Behind the scampering came footsteps. There was a *scratch, scratch, scratching* at my bedroom door.

I ran to open it, and Poochie leaped past me and onto the bed.

"Please let her stay," I begged.

Dad stood, looking down at us. "Tommy and Poochie. I'm telling you both now. This is the very last time. You hear me, Tom?"

I nodded.

He wasn't kidding. The next night they let poor Poochie cry and cry.

"Don't worry," Dad said. "She'll get used to it. We just have to be firm."

Poochie cried all that night and all the next night, too.

"She'll get sick," I told Mom and Dad.

"A puppy needs her sleep."

Dad rubbed his eyes. "What about a mom and dad? They need their sleep, too," he said.

The next night Mom wound up an old-fashioned clock and put it in Poochie's basket.

"I read somewhere that she'll think the ticking of the clock is her mother's heartbeat," Mom said. "She'll be so happy, she'll purr."

"Puppies don't purr," I told her. "Cats purr."

"Whatever," Mom said. "I'm so tired, I don't remember the difference."

Poochie didn't purr. She knew that clock wasn't her mother. She cried louder than ever.

"We could carry Poochie's Place up to Tommy's room," Mom suggested.

Dad shook his head. "One second later she'd hop out of her basket and into Tommy's bed. That's not a good idea."

The next night Mom put a hot water bottle in Poochie's basket. "A hot water bottle is supposed to make her sleep," she said.

It didn't.

Dad sat on the floor next to the basket and held Poochie's paw while he sang her a lullaby.

It was the dumbest song I'd ever heard. Fortunately, Dad soon fell asleep.

While Dad slept, Poochie jumped over him to come to me. I smoothed Dad's nice bald head. "Poor, tired Daddy," I said.

"I think Poochie was very nice to wait until Dad almost finished his song," Mom said in a small voice.

14

When Dad woke up he yawned. "That's the longest and best sleep I've had all week," he muttered. "Take Poochie up with you, Tommy. Mom and I have to get some rest. Tomorrow we'll think of something else to try. I don't know what. But something."

Chapter Three
I Think This
Is the Answer

The next morning Mrs. Cavan, our
next-door neighbor, came to our house.
She and Mom had a talk, and she gave
Mom an idea. I think Mrs. Cavan could
hear Poochie barking at night, too.
She's probably pretty desperate, herself.

She brought Mom a big mirror.

"I had this stored in my attic," she said. "Put it in Poochie's basket. She'll think it's another puppy."

Mom was really pleased. She put the mirror in the basket. Poochie wriggled across to it, put her nose to the glass, and then wriggled away again. Poochie was not fooled.

"That was a good idea," Dad said. "But I think a mirror is too hard. She knows that another puppy would be soft and warm."

That day he went to the store and bought a cuddly stuffed toy dog. I had to admit, it was pretty cute and pretty lifelike.

"I think this is the answer," Dad said happily, putting the stuffed toy in the basket next to Poochie.

Poochie chewed its ear, batted it with her paw, and then ignored it. And that night she cried just as much as ever.

Mrs. Cavan came over the next morning. She brought Poochie a nice little rubber bone she'd bought in the market.

"Please, Poochie," Mrs. Cavan said. "You are disrupting the neighborhood."

I wasn't sure what *disrupting* meant. But it didn't sound good.

Dad looked grim. "We're at the end of our patience," he told Mrs. Cavan.

"I'm sorry Poochie is being such a pest. We'd take her back, but Tommy..." He stopped and glanced at me. I knew he meant that I'd be heartbroken if they took Poochie back.

I *would* be heartbroken. Absolutely and forever heartbroken. I put my arms tight around Poochie and kissed her head.

"I won't let that happen," I whispered.

Chapter Four
It Must Be Magic

Poochie and I sat together in the garden and thought and thought.

We talked for a long time.

"We've got to convince them that your place is with me all the time, day and night," I said. "Sometimes it's hard to

make grown-ups change their minds.
That's because they're usually right.
But not this time."

We thought and thought, and then I
said, "I've got it, Poochie! I've got it!"

That night, Poochie was yelping in the
kitchen. I got up and went quietly down
the deep, dark stairs. The hall clock
struck midnight. I wished I had my dog
right beside me. There might be monsters.

Poochie was so glad to see me. I was
glad to see her, too. She watched as I
unhooked the sign from above the door
of her doggie house. She came with me
as I dragged the sign up the stairs. Even
though I had her to protect me, I was
still scared. Poochie's not very big.
Monsters can be humongous. I went as
fast as I could. But it was hard because
I was dragging the sign.

From Mom and Dad's room came two sets of snores—one deep, one whistling.

Hink, grr, honk, grr, hink, whee, honk, whee. I was really glad they were tired enough to sleep.

I carried the sign over to my bed and laid it on the comforter. It slid off with an awful bump. And—oh my gosh—the bump had awakened Mom and Dad. I quickly lifted the sign back onto the comforter.

"Quick," I told Poochie, "they're coming!"

We were pretending to be asleep when Mom and Dad opened my door. I heard them come over to my bed.

"Oh, my," Mom said, and she began to laugh. "How did that sign get up here?" she asked Dad.

I opened one eye and saw Dad

scratching his head. "For sure, Tommy and Poochie didn't carry it up. Now it's here and Poochie's here."

"Besides," Mom said, "they're fast asleep."

"It must be magic," Dad said. "The magic is trying to tell us something, so I guess we'd better pay attention. Sometimes it's smart to know when to give up. Those little guys want to be together so much, I don't have the heart to keep them separate anymore." His voice was soft.

Mom stroked my hair. "And you were so brave to go all the way down the stairs in the dark," she whispered.

I almost said, "I know," but then I remembered I was supposed to be asleep.

"OK, then," Dad said. He tucked the covers around Poochie and me and kissed us. I secretly squeezed Poochie's paw.

The next day, Dad hung the Poochie's Place sign above my bed. Poochie and I jumped all around the room.

After breakfast, we watched Dad carry Poochie's basket into the back yard.

"Good riddance," I whispered. Poochie wagged her tail.

But then the nicest thing happened.

Mom was standing by the window. "Tommy, Come and see," she whispered.

There, in Poochie's basket, was a mother opossum and her three babies, bundled together and sleeping in a warm little circle.

"That mama opossum has been walking around our yard a lot," Mom said. "I think she was looking for a nice house for her little ones. Now she's found it."

"We definitely need a new sign," Dad

said. "I'll make one tomorrow."

And he did.

Possum's Place, the sign says. And it hangs right above Poochie's old basket.